celebrating
australia

Steve Parish™
PUBLISHING

Preceding pages: A solitary gum tree rises above the scrub; Sydney Harbour Bridge frames the Opera House, NSW; Uluru, Northern Territory.   *Above:* A Koala snoozes in the fork of a gum tree.

Introduction

There are few travel restrictions in Australia, no internal customs, no passport to produce when leaving one State or Territory for another. One currency is in use throughout the continent, and one language is understood by nearly all its inhabitants, from Darwin to Hobart, Perth to Sydney, Alice Springs to Lord Howe Island.

This mighty continent is made for adventuring, for it is full of natural marvels and unique plants and animals. There are primeval rainforests, awesome deserts, rugged, snow-capped ranges and a coastline of scenic splendours. The Great Barrier Reef, with its teeming marine life and enchanting islands, extends for 2000 kilometres along the north-eastern coast, and on the other side of the country are the dolphins and dugongs of Shark Bay. It is not necessary to travel far from the major cities to encounter fantastic landforms such as the Twelve Apostles in Victoria or the Three Sisters in New South Wales. Longer, well-planned adventures are safe and rewarding. A few hours' drive takes the traveller from Darwin to Kakadu, a few hours in a plane brings the majestic sight of Uluru, that breathtaking rock in the centre of the continent.

Australia's cities are safe places to stroll, to savour the sights and to enjoy great meals and sophisticated shopping and entertainment. Country towns offer their own delights, from warm hospitality to historic buildings and a taste of life on the land outback.

This is my Australia, and I spend as much time as I can wandering its highways and byways, always finding new places to see and new sights to record on film. This book brings together some of my favourite images, and as I turn its pages I relive the emotions that each place and each person aroused in me. I hope you enjoy this celebration of the country I love, and that it conveys my passion for this very special land.

Steve Parish

AUSTRALIA – a vast land

Looking over Middle Harbour, to the city centre of Sydney, New South Wales.

Australia covers 7 682 300 square kilometres and has a population of over 17 million. The coastline is approximately 36 000 kilometres in length and the distance between the most easterly and most westerly points of the continent is about 4000 kilometres. All major Australian cities, except for Canberra, are on the coast.

The majestic sandstone ramparts of the Arnhem Land Escarpment, Kakadu National Park, Northern Territory.

Australia has 6500 areas, ranging from a few hectares to thousands of square kilometres, named as national parks and other conservation reserves. Together they make up almost ten percent of the continent. They are vital areas for the nation's physical and spiritual wellbeing, and are places of pilgrimage and adventure for Australians and overseas visitors alike.

A land of contrasts

A snow gum in the wintry Australian Alps, highest section of the Great Dividing Range.

The awesome sand dunes of the Simpson, one of Australia's central deserts.

Australia's major mountain chain, the Great Dividing Range, runs down the continent's east coast. To the east of the Divide are forests and coastal plains; to the west, the land becomes increasingly arid and contains some of the world's great deserts. The extreme north of Australia is monsoonal, while the south-west has a Mediterranean climate. These diverse climates have created landscapes of enormous contrast.

4

The Low Isles, cays which have risen on coral platforms on the Great Barrier Reef.

The spectacular Chalahn Falls in the subtropical rainforest of Lamington National Park.

LANDSCAPE ICONS OF AUSTRALIA

Photographers wait to record the moment when Uluru glows crimson in the dawn light

What makes a landscape feature so memorable that millions regard it as symbolic of the country in which it stands? It is not ease of access – some of Australia's landscape icons are far from easy to reach, though public demand has ensured their inclusion in travel itineraries. It is not necessarily immediate impact, though the "Wow!" factor applies to many. Perhaps it is their appeal to our human need for images of magic – pillars of stone defy the elements, islands are born in coral seas, water cascades in awesome thunder and rainforest clothes the earth in primal splendour.

Lady Musgrave Island, Great Barrier Reef Marine Park, Queensland.

Jim Jim Falls, Kakadu National Park, Northern Territory.

The Three Sisters, Blue Mountains National Park, New South Wales.

The Twelve Apostles, Port Campbell National Park, Victoria.

Above: Belmore Falls, Morton National Park, New South Wales.

Above: Mt Kosciusko, Kosciusko National Park, New South Wales.

Icons of New South Wales

In 1788, New South Wales was the site of first European settlement in Australia. The State occupies one-tenth of the area of Australia and has four major natural zones: a coastal plain, the mountains of the Great Dividing Range, the gentle western slopes of the Divide and extensive western plains.

Many of New South Wales's best-loved landscape features are in the Great Dividing Range. To the north, the seaward slopes are dissected by wild rivers and harbour magnificent areas of rainforest. Near Sydney, the scenic Blue Mountains rise in sandstone splendour. Further south are the Australian Alps, with majestic High Country peaks.

Opposite: Sightseers in the Skyway aerial railcar have a splendid view of the Three Sisters and the Jamison Valley in the Blue Mountains National Park, New South Wales.

Home from the sea: a peaceful scene on Lord Howe Island, a World Heritage Area, 700 km from Sydney, New South Wales.

The solid cores of ancient volcanoes in Warrumbungle National Park, New South Wales.

Above: Cool temperate rainforest splendour in Tarra-Bulga National Park, Victoria.

Icons of Victoria

Victoria occupies an area slightly less than that of the United Kingdom, approximately 227 600 square kilometres. For its size, it has an enormous diversity of scenery, from the dry mallee country of the Murray River Basin in the north to the rugged coastal mountains and forests of the Otway Ranges west of Melbourne and South Gippsland east of the city. Wilsons Promontory, part of these southern uplands, is the southernmost point of mainland Australia.

The Great Dividing Range runs east-west across Victoria, rising to nearly 2000 metres in the Victorian Alps. The Divide's western extremity is the spectacular Grampians of the Central Highlands district.

Opposite: The Twelve Apostles, Port Campbell National Park, Victoria.

Above: The most southerly peninsula on the mainland, Wilsons Promontory, Victoria.

The Balconies, also called the Jaws of Death, Grampians National Park, Victoria.

The breathtaking beauty of the High Country of the Victorian Alps, Alpine National Park, Victoria.

Icons of Queensland

Above and opposite: The flat, dry stretches of the Simpson Desert National Park are in stark contrast to the tropical vegetation of Whitsunday Island.

Second largest of the Australian States, with the largest habitable area, Queensland occupies the north-eastern quarter of the continent. It has a wide range of climatic types and landscapes and its eastern coastline showcases not only subtropical and tropical rainforest but also the unique sand mass of Fraser Island and, further north, the 2000 kilometres of coral reefs and cays that make up the remarkable Great Barrier Reef.

West of the Great Dividing Range, a number of rivers run south-west, first through grassy plains and then across the drier Channel Country. After rain, the outback, including the south-western Simpson Desert, blossoms into life.

Tropical rainforest in the Wet Tropics World Heritage wilderness of the Daintree National Park, North Queensland.

18

Green Island, a coral cay in the Great Barrier Reef Marine Park, off Cairns, North Queensland.

Icons of the Northern Territory

Glen Helen Gorge, in West MacDonnell National Park near Alice Springs, Northern Territory.

The coastline of the Northern Territory, excluding its islands, is about 5100 kilometres long, and it occupies around one-sixth of mainland Australia. The northern part of the Territory, called the Top End, is bordered by mangrove swamps and coastal wetlands bounded in the south by the massive sandstone Arnhem Land Escarpment, edge of an extensive plateau. The south of the Territory is dominated by ranges of granite, sandstone and quartzite, separated by sand and stony plains. The rugged MacDonnell Ranges run east–west, rising to 1511 metres above sea level.

Wangi Falls, tumbling over the sandstone of Litchfield National Park, Northern Territory.

Nitmiluk, carved in stone by the Katherine River, south of Darwin, Northern Territory.

Twin Falls, a memorable sight in the Wet in Kakadu National Park, Northern Territory.

Yellow Water, in the coastal wetlands of Kakadu National Park, Northern Territory.

Uluṟu, a magnificent sight in the Central Australian desert, especially at sunrise and sunset, Uluṟu–Kata Tjuṯa National Park, Northern Territory.

Some of the many domes of Kata Tjuṯa, a group of gigantic rock formations which stands in Uluṟu–Kata Tjuṯa National Park, Northern Territory.

Wave Rock, a towering crest of granite near Hyden, in the area of Western Australia known as the wheat belt.

The majestic, striped sandstone turrets of the Bungle Bungles, Purnululu National Park, Western Australia.

Icons of Western Australia

Occupying one-third of Australia's land-mass, Western Australia stretches for around 2400 kilometres from the Kimberley in the north to the scenic southern coast. A little more than one-third lies within the tropics. Most is a plateau standing between 300 and 600 metres above sea-level.

Some of Western Australia's rock formations are among the oldest known on Earth. It is not surprising that many of its best-known landmarks involve rocks or stones, including the icons shown here. The most notable Western Australian mountains are the Kimberley's King Leopold Range, once a coral reef, the north-west's enormous Mt Augustus, the largest monolith in the world, the rugged, iron-rich Hamersley Range of the Pilbara, and the Stirling Range and Porongorups, north of Albany on the south coast.

The Pinnacles, aggregations of limestone formed underground and exposed by erosion in Nambung National Park, Western Australia.

Landscape-framing Nature's Window, in Kalbarri National Park, shows clearly the layers of rock originally laid down as silt and mud under an ancient sea.

The Salmon Holes, Torndirrup National Park, a secluded sandy beach and jutting granite headland typical of the southern coastline of Western Australia.

The massive slopes of Mt Augustus, the world's largest rock, rise majestically from the plains in Mt Augustus National Park.

Remarkable Rocks, weathered granite boulders in Kangaroo Island's Flinders Chase National Park, South Australia.

Icons of South Australia

Tanunda, gateway to the the wineries and vineyards of the Barossa Valley.

Weathered peaks in the Flinders Ranges National Park, South Australia.

South Australia's area represents an eighth of the Australian continent. About half of the State is less than 150 metres above sea level and it is largely flat, so the ranges which comprise the Mt Lofty-Flinders Ranges system stand in startling relief from the surrounding plains. This is the driest State, whose only large permanent river is the Murray. However, the fertile south-east, including Adelaide, the capital city, is blessed with a Mediterranean climate, and yields, among other produce, magnificent wine grapes.

The rugged Arthur Range and a cirque lake, in the wilderness of South West National Park, Tasmania.

Icons of Tasmania

Smallest of Australia's six States, Tasmania is a roughly triangular island divided from the mainland by Bass Strait. It accounts for nearly one-tenth of the total area of Australia. The capital city, Hobart, is the southernmost of Australia's capitals, and the second oldest after Sydney.

Tasmania contains stunning examples of wilderness, notably in the south-west. In 1982, the World Heritage Commission listed the area, which encompasses Wild Rivers, South West, Cradle Mountain–Lake St Clair and Walls of Jerusalem National Parks.

In stark contrast is the farmland of the east, dotted with towns and villages whose history is lovingly preserved.

Russell Falls, in the marvellous temperate rainforest of Mt Field National Park, easily accessible from Hobart, capital of Tasmania.

Jagged, weathered peaks in Cradle Mountain–Lake St Clair National Park, Tasmania.

THE NATION'S CAPITAL CITIES

Although Australia is a huge continent, most of its population is to be found in the capital cities of its six States and two Territories. The distances between these cities are enormous compared to distances between centres of population in many other countries. However, the cities themselves were founded by people of largely similar origins, cultures and beliefs. All were placed near water sources and all but Canberra began as working ports, or in close association with ports. Thus they share some similar features.

However, Australia's capitals were established in three different centuries, and for quite different purposes. Sydney was founded in 1788 for the purpose of punishing convicts transported from the British Isles. As the nineteenth century progressed, it became a place where free settlers and emancipists could make their fortunes, and for many years it ruled the penal settlements at Hobart and Brisbane, and the free settlement of Melbourne. All three had to establish their identities as States and win the right to govern themselves. Perth and Adelaide began as free colonies (though Perth later accepted convict labour), and were bastions of private enterprise. Darwin was the last capital established in the nineteenth century and still is the major centre of a Territory rather than a State. Canberra, founded in 1913 and designed to be the national capital, has not been subject to the cycles of boom, bust and regrowth which mineral discoveries – gold, silver, copper and iron in particular – have brought to the other capitals.

History, geography, patterns of immigration and the impact of the exploitation of natural resources have given Australia's capital cities magnificently separate identities. Airports and hotel chains apart, they are places where the traveller can look around and say with certainty, "This is Melbourne!" or "Here I am in Perth (or Hobart, or Adelaide, or Darwin, Sydney, Canberra or Brisbane)."

The images on the following pages are typical of the nation's major cities.

Opposite: The Opera House and the Harbour Bridge, in Sydney, capital of New South Wales.

Images of Canberra

A mosaic expressing an Aboriginal theme of "people meeting for a ceremony" distinguishes the forecourt of Parliament House, Canberra.

Fountains and facade of the High Court of Australia.

The imposing Australian National Gallery.

Canberra's buildings did not appear gradually over generations, responding to the needs of their users. They were designed to house the nation's great institutions, and to present impressive outward appearances and grand interiors. The High Court and National Gallery are beautifully situated on the shores of Lake Burley Griffin.

Images of Sydney

A view across Bondi, Sydney's most famous beach, to city and harbour.

Sydney, capital of New South Wales, is centred on the magnificent Sydney Harbour. Largest city of Australia, it has a population of nearly four million people and is internationally recognised as one of the world's great cities. On the 26th of January 1788, the Union Jack was raised on the shores of Sydney Cove in a ceremony conducted by Captain Arthur Phillip, commander of the First Fleet which brought 1023 souls to Australia, including 751 convicts. Sydney now stretches from the Tasman Sea westwards to the Blue Mountains, and from Royal National Park northwards to the Hawkesbury River. It contains many marvels of engineering, construction and design, including the Harbour Bridge, Opera House and Queen Victoria Building and such splendid beaches as Bondi and Manly and Coogee.

Opposite: Three symbols of Sydney – Harbour, Bridge and Opera House.
Following pages: An aerial view of Sydney over Kirribilli.

Reflections of the gilded towers of Melbourne at dawn are broken as rowers glide down the Yarra.

Images of Melbourne

Second-largest city in Australia, Melbourne is the capital of Victoria, with a population of more than three million people. It stands at the mouth of the Yarra River, on the shores of Port Phillip Bay. Settled in 1835 by colonists from Tasmania led by John Batman, Melbourne was officially named in 1837, and by 1851 Victoria was proclaimed a separate colony. The prosperity that followed the gold rushes of the 1850s put Marvellous Melbourne on its feet. Today, it is an elegant city which values its history while moving confidently to the future. Noted for its multicultural population, for the excellence of its food and wine, and as a venue for the arts, Melbourne is a sophisticated city of international renown.

Opposite: Domed Flinders Street Station, a Melbourne landmark.
Following pages: An aerial view over Melbourne to Port Phillip Bay.

Cray boats and cruisers occupy berths used by the Sydney to Hobart yachts at the end of their ocean race.

Images of Hobart

Ninth-largest and second-oldest city in Australia, Hobart, founded in 1804, is the capital of Tasmania, with a population of nearly 200 000. Built on the banks of the Derwent River with Mt Wellington as backdrop, Hobart is a beautiful, prosperous city which prizes its historic buildings dating from the convict era. Its superb harbour is important to the commercial life of Hobart and is the final mooring of yachts in the bluewater classic Sydney to Hobart race.

Opposite: Looking over the city of Hobart to the Derwent River.
Following pages: Wrest Point Casino stands in front of river and suburbs.

Images of Adelaide

Above: Glenelg jetty, close to where the first settlers landed to found Adelaide.　　　*Opposite:* The city of Adelaide, with Torrens Lake and the Festival Centre at the centre.

The capital of South Australia, Adelaide is the fifth-largest city of Australia, with a population of about a million. It stands on the fertile plains of the Torrens River, on the eastern shore of St Vincents Gulf and is bounded on the landward side by the Mt Lofty Ranges.

South Australia was founded in 1836 as a colony for free settlers, who had to be able to purchase land there. Adelaide was laid out following the far-sighted plan of Surveyor-General Colonel William Light. It is a splendidly spacious city, whose Festival of Arts, held every second year, has established it as an important cultural centre. The climate and soil suit viticulture, and the wines of the area are famous.

The fountain designed by John Dowie for Victoria Square symbolises three rivers.

Glenelg Town Hall in Moseley Square, near the Adelaide–Glenelg tram terminal.

Adelaide has managed to retain some of its historic buildings, and even adapt them to the pace of modern workaday existence, while constructing new ones in keeping with the city's charm. Where else in the world would a railway station amiably share working space with a casino? Colonel Light's vision created an elegant, cultured city bounded by wide terraces and surrounded by parklands.

Adelaide Railway Station, on North Terrace, also houses the Adelaide Casino.

An evening view of Adelaide city across Torrens Lake.

Looking westwards down Hay Street Mall.

Images of Perth

Perth, capital of Western Australia, was founded in 1829. It stands between the Indian Ocean and the escarpment known as the Darling Range, on the lower courses of the Swan and the Canning Rivers. The city centre is 16 kilometres from the mouth of the Swan, which runs to the sea at the port of Fremantle.

Australia's fourth-largest city, Perth has a population of more than a million people. It enjoys a Mediterranean climate, providing conditions ideal for outdoor amusements and venues such as the famous Hay Street and Murray Street Malls in the city. Kings Park, a reserve on Mt Eliza, overlooks the city and the Swan River, and houses spectacular wildflower gardens. Perth is also famous for its magnificent ocean beaches, which run north and south of the city.

Opposite: Perth from the air, with a view to the distant Darling Range.

Scarborough Beach, dominated by the tower of Observation City, is one of Perth's closest beaches.

56

The Narrows Bridge over the Swan River joins South Perth to Perth city.

Above: Relaxing on Mindil Beach, in front of Mindil Markets, during the Beer Can Regatta.

Images of Darwin

Capital of the Northern Territory, Darwin, with a population of around 80 000, is the fourteenth-largest city of Australia. Founded in 1869 after several attempts at selecting a site, it occupies a peninsula jutting into Beagle Gulf, with Frances Bay on the east side and Fannie Bay on the west. Space has never been a problem in Darwin, and it is a sprawling city extending around a vast airport, civil and military. Its climate is tropical: the average maximum temperature in all 12 months exceeds 30°C. The middle months of the year are pleasantly warm and dry; the Wet, which breaks in November/December and lasts until March, brings torrential rains which invigorate plant and animal life. Life in Darwin centres around outdoor activities, and the city's gardens are outstanding. Dining on the Wharf Precinct, strolling on the Esplanade and joining festivities such as Mindil Markets are splendid pleasures of Darwin life.

Opposite: An aerial view of Darwin, with the Esplanade on the right and the Wharf Precinct near the top.

Above: This cartoon cousin of the saltwater crocodile welcomes tourists to observe its wild relatives in safety.

Images of Brisbane

Brisbane's towers stand tall beyond homes built on stilts for coolness.

Opposite: Brisbane's central business district, seen over the Brisbane River.

Brisbane, subtropical capital of Queensland, covers a very large area and, with a population of about 1.4 million, is the third-largest city in Australia. First established in 1826 as a settlement to take the most intractable of convicts, it stands on the tidal lower course of the mighty Brisbane River as it flows into Moreton Bay. As the outer fringes of the city extend north and south along the coastal plain, many residents are choosing to move to the inner suburbs and refurbish traditional Queensland timber houses with corrugated iron roofs. Brisbane Forest Park, 26 500 hectares of bushland, is within easy reach of the city, as are the world-famous beaches of the Gold and Sunshine Coasts.

Kodak Beach, a playground complete with lifeguard, at South Bank Parklands, across the Brisbane River from the city centre.

Brisbane's Riverside Centre and Eagle Street Pier, where cruise paddlewheelers and other craft are moored. This area hosts popular Sunday markets.

Painting of man and two large ground-feeding birds, in ochre on rock.

Painting of monitor lizard, in ochre on rock.

Symbols pecked into rock.

Hand stencils made by spraying ochre onto rock.

Wandjina figures from the Keep River National Park, Northern Territory.

THE LAND AND ITS PEOPLE

The first Australians

The Aboriginal people of Australia have lived on the continent for at least 50 000 years, and may have been resident for far longer. Long-lasting records of their association with the country in which they lived were made on walls of rock. Some paintings were made far back in time, beyond the traditions of any modern living group of Aboriginal people.

The places in which rock paintings are made have always been locations of significance in their own right. Some paintings depicted ancestral figures, some were of prey animals, renewed at intervals to ensure a plentiful supply of food. Red, black, yellow and white pigments were used for rock art throughout Australia. Often these were traded over long distances. If not constantly renewed, the fragile paintings are easily damaged by weather, insects, rubbing and licking by larger animals, and human vandalism.

Intricate dotted patterns, and magnificently detailed X-ray figures are elements which have brought international fame to the Aboriginal art of Australia.

Above: The DIG tree, Cooper Creek, a reminder of the fate of explorers Burke, Wills and Gray in 1861.

The gibber desert of Central Australia – country inhospitable to travellers.

The coming of Europeans

The Dutch captains whose vessels grazed the coast of Western Australia in the seventeenth century were not interested in settlement of this southern continent. They were simply using winds and currents to make a faster landfall in the East Indies. After the government of Great Britain decided to claim New Holland as an alternative to England's prisons, in 1788, active exploration was discouraged as unsettling to the convicts. However, free settlers wanted land, and once the barrier of the Blue Mountains had been overcome in 1813 exploration continued, encouraged by the desire for fertile fields and pastures, and for gold. There was always the drive to see what lay beyond the horizon, and expeditions were regularly mounted to map the country not yet surveyed. Some succeeded, some perished, for the nature of the country was not understood. Settlers and squatters who established farms in good seasons were often forced from the land when inappropriate agricultural practices, better suited to Europe's deep, fertile soils, and the vagaries of the Australian climate worked against them.

A monument to shattered dreams, in an area of Australia which suffers from recurrent droughts.

The city canyons of Sydney, a bustling international business centre which still is very Australian.

Australians today

Australia was colonised by the British, but rapidly assimilated newcomers from most of the world's nations. The gold rushes which began in the early 1850s brought a flood of immigrants from all over the world, including China and the United States of America, and many of these adventurers remained after the lust for gold faded. Today, Australia's more than 17 million people come from many ethnic and cultural backgrounds. Secure in their identity as Australians, cultural groups take pride in maintaining their traditions, and generously share their cultural inheritance in public celebrations such as parades and festivals. As modern means of communications and travel overcome the isolation so keenly felt by the first European settlers, Australians proudly take their place in the global village. Artists and artisans, writers and thinkers, people of the cities and the outback, people of sport and business, all play their part in the richness of Australian life.

The young people taking part in this colourful display during Darwin's annual festival emphasise the harmonious meeting of cultures.

Bringing the mob to market along a country road, in outback Queensland.

Sharpening the knife to cut cane the old way. Today, most cane is cut by machines.

Australians love to work the land

In a land blessed with a wealth of natural resources, but where distances are vast, soils easily exhausted and climates unpredictable, Australians have traditionally worked hard to make a living from the soil, the pastures, the forests and the seas. Today, wise farmers and pastoralists put back what their crops and stock take from the land. Aquaculture is helping to replenish marine resources depleted by fishing. The forestry industry replants as it takes out timber, and miners protect and regenerate the environment. Mechanisation has taken much of the "hard yakka" out of working the land, but physical skills and determination are still needed for most tasks. It's not always an easy life, but few country people want to live in town and, from the cray boats of Western Australia to the cane farms of coastal Queensland, they usually think their way of life beats all others.

The kind of work known as "hard yakka", at a mine at Coolgardie, Western Australia.

Drying apricots, in the Sunraysia area of the Murray River, Victoria.

Shearing the wethers, on a hot day in the outback of New South Wales.

Bringing in the pot, Lake Alexandrina, South Australia.

A portrait gallery from outback Australia.

Australians love the footy

Football is a consuming passion with Australians of all ages, sexes and occupations. The code of football may differ: New South Wales, Queensland and the Australian Capital Territory are mad about Rugby Union and Rugby League; Australian Rules, traditionally played in the southern States, is now a national code in which most States vie for each year's Holy Grail of the Australian Football League Premiership; soccer, which attracts many Australian star players to overseas careers, has an increasing hold on the public imagination.

Left: Australian Football League teams' colours at the opening ceremony of the Aussie Rules Centenary Grand Final at the packed Melbourne Cricket Ground in 1996.

Australians love the Cup

Horse-racing has traditionally had an enthusiastic following in Australia – by 1802 there were 300 horses in the colony, including the thoroughbred stallion Northumberland, and racing had begun. The Melbourne Cup, held since 1861, is only one of many horse races to take place every year in Australia, but it is the richest, with prize money of more than a million dollars. It is also the only contest that literally "stops the nation". On the first Tuesday in November, millions of Australians may be found turning on the television or the radio or joining the other 100 000 punters crowding the fences and stands at Melbourne's Flemington Racecourse to watch one gallant thoroughbred head the field and come thundering down the straight to turf immortality.

Right: Past the post in the Melbourne Cup, a turf classic held at Flemington.

Australians love the cricket

Two teams of eleven, two umpires, two sets of wickets, a strip of more or less grassed earth and a small, hard ball. Add spectators ranging in number from a couple of parents and friends to the enormous crowd shown in this picture of the Sydney Cricket Ground and you have an Australian cricket match. What cannot be shown in any photograph is the enthusiasm and expertise with which Australians support their local, State and National teams.

Left: Sydney Cricket Ground during a day-night International.

Surfing is a year-round sport for many Australians.

Exploring the mysteries and marvels of the Great Barrier Reef.

Australians love the sea

Australians living far from an ocean beach look forward to spending their holidays at the seaside: Australians living near the coastline – all 36 000 kilometres of it – take access to the sea for granted. They swim in it, dive into its depths, surf its waves, take fish from its waters, sail, paddle and powerboat across its surface. They watch whales swimming in it, walk its sands and at times simply sit along its shores, watching the waves and listening to their endless music.

Opposite: Bondi, internationally-known symbol of Australia's beaches.

Ocean-going sailing vessels jostle for position as they fly across Sydney Harbour at the beginning of the annual Sydney to Hobart Yacht Race.

Above: Fishing off the beach at Cooloola, on Queensland's Sunshine Coast.

Following pages: Queensland's Gold Coast, where the world enjoys Australian sea, sand and surf.

In freshness and variety, Australian food is of the finest, and it is prepared and served by skilled, friendly people in pleasant surroundings.

Australians love to shop

Back in colonial days, barter was the way to obtain necessities. Today, Australians use cash and, increasingly, plastic cards to make purchases, but the friendly atmosphere of the marketplace still survives. Australian-manufactured products are known for good design and durability. Boutiques and department stores display racks of Australian-made garments whose quality and elegance rival any imported goods, while Australia's butcheries, greengroceries, fruit shops, bakeries, seafood shops and delicatessens sell wares unequalled for quality and freshness.

Boutiques offer Australian-made and imported women's and men's clothes.

For the grand city mansion or homely country cottage, furnishings and decorations aplenty are to be found by the dedicated shopper.

Greeting friends and exchanging the news of the day.

Promoting the conservation of endangered native animals.

Sharing Aboriginality with a young audience.

Making the crowds laugh.

Australians love an audience

An old bushy with a twinkle in his eye wields the squeeze-box.

Oral traditions run strong in Australian life, from the custom of swapping yarns with mates at the pub, in the club or, increasingly, at an open-air café, to more formal occasions – for instance, making a speech at a wedding. The right of free speech is taken seriously in this democratic country, but Australians generally are an irreverent mob, and "taking the mickey" is a national pastime. While this country has produced world-class professional entertainers and performers, ordinary folk entertain themselves and others with stories and music, jokes and poems, and the larrikins need no second invitation to take centre stage. And they start young: at home, excited children organise concerts to entertain family and friends, or take to the stage, more or less eagerly, at school concerts.

Australians love to be outdoors

Fishing Pumicestone Passage between Bribie Island and mainland Queensland as the sun sinks behind the Glasshouse Mountains.

There are very few places in Australia where it is impossible to spend time outdoors. Even in the coldest winter in Tasmania's highlands, there are days of brilliant sunshine, and summer is delightful. Even in the hottest summer in the Red Centre, nightfall brings a million stars in a velvet sky, and winter is cool and pleasant.

Most of the time, Australia is a safe and rewarding place to work or play outdoors. It is a paradise for adventurers, nature lovers, bushwalkers, beachgoers, those who love messing about with boats and anyone who enjoys breathing fresh air and discovering a new vista at every turn of the road.

Enjoying the outdoor life in Kakadu National Park, Northern Territory.

Some choose to make the lengthy climb to the summit of Uluṟu, in the Northern Territory.

Tasmania's magnificent south-western wilderness is mecca for bushwalkers.

The sand dunes of Queensland's Simpson Desert are best explored by the hardy and wary.

Australians love to be creative

The bathing boxes at Brighton, Melbourne, and a fine work of performance art.

Folk art is alive and well in Australia. With determination and lots of creativity, the most unpromising materials can be turned into works of art. Take the motor tyres and galvanised iron used to such effect in the garden of the Jericho home opposite: water is scarce, so the true beauty of the garden lies in the effort which has gone into creating it. The same could be said of the sculptured Australian crest, created by lonely men after long hours of back-breaking labour. The Brighton beach boxes are works of art in themselves. The ceremonial burial just adds an unposed and effective touch.

A menagerie decorates a lovingly tended front garden in Jericho, Queensland.

Above: Patriotic bas-relief, fettlers' camp on the Old Ghan Railway, South Australia.   *Following pages:* Works of art in the streets of Silverton, New South Wales.

The Australian War Memorial and Museum in Canberra.

Australians do not forget

Australians have taken an active part in ten armed conflicts since 1860. In all of them, Australian men and women served gallantly and in all of them, Australians gave their lives, from the unknown number who did not return from reinforcing British troops in New Zealand in the Maori Wars, 1845–72, to the 60 454 deaths in World War I, and the 39 450 killed in World War II. These figures do not include those taken prisoner or wounded in action.

Around Australia, quiet crowds gather on two solemn occasions each year, first on the 25th of April for the Anzac Day ceremonies which commemorate the dead of Gallipoli, a major action of World War I in which battalions of Australian and New Zealand troops were killed. This service has been extended to serve as a memorial to those who served their country in all wars. Remembrance Day, on the 11th of November each year, commemorates the signing of the armistice to end World War I in 1918, pays tribute to those who fell in time of war and unites the nation in one minute's silent reflection, which begins at the eleventh hour of the day.

Much decorated servicemen remembering those who did not return.

A mother Koala and her joey are cared for in a wildlife sanctuary.

Australians love Koalas

The Koala spends most of its life in the branches of a tree, preferably a eucalypt, and eats nothing but leaves. It sleeps for much of the time and is generally most active at night. It has become a much loved, universally recognised symbol of Australia, and it is actually easier to find a Koala in a wildlife sanctuary than out in the bush. Much of the eastern coastal eucalypt forest in which it prefers to live has been cleared, and Koala conservation depends on preservation of its home.

Opposite: The endearing Koala, a marsupial symbol of Australia.

These two young wombats have been hand-reared after their mothers were victims of cars or dogs.

Meeting a wombat is a thrill for a young nature lover.

Australians love wombats

There are three sorts of wombat in Australia, two of them very rare. The most familiar sort, the Common Wombat, is found in forested country in south-eastern Australia. It has a powerful build with short legs and broad paws tipped with strong claws ideally suited to digging. A number of wombats may live in a communal burrow, each with its own living space. They sleep during the day and emerge at night to feed on grasses and roots. A female wombat has a pouch which opens to the rear. Her young one is carried in her pouch while she digs and forages.

Opposite: A Common Wombat eating grass. Note its strong digging claws.

Australians love kangaroos

Above: An orphaned Pretty-face Wallaby rides in a substitute for mother's pouch.

Above: The children are delighted, but the big male Red Kangaroo just wants to sleep.
Opposite: An Eastern Grey Kangaroo joey peeps from its mother's pouch.

There are all sorts, sizes, shapes and colours of kangaroos. The smaller ones are called wallabies, and the smallest of all are called potoroos. Red Kangaroos live on plains and in aridlands, while Grey Kangaroos prefer wetter, more forested country. All give birth to tiny naked young, which are carried in their mothers' pouches until they can live independently. The kangaroo is represented on Australia's coat of arms.

Australians love birds

The Laughing Kookaburra is famous for its loud, rollicking, laugh-like call.

The Emu is one of the faunal symbols of the Commonwealth of Australia.

There are around 760 different sorts of birds to be seen in Australia and on the seas around its shores. Some sorts of birds are found nowhere else in the world, and Australia is sometimes called "the land of parrots" because it is home to so many different species of these brightly feathered gems. Other remarkable groups are the bowerbirds and lyrebirds.

One of the best-known brown-feathered birds is the Laughing Kookaburra whose family groups proclaim their territory in loud, chuckling choruses at dawn. The other is the Emu. This, the world's second-tallest bird, is flightless, and has only feathery flaps instead of wings.

The Crimson Rosella, a parrot of eastern forested mountain ranges.

Overrun by parrots which flock for handouts in a National Park camping ground.

Feeding Rainbow Lorikeets, fast-flying parrots which normally eat nectar.

The male Australian King-Parrot is one of Australia's most vividly coloured birds.

Getting into the mood of a past age at the George Street Festival in Brisbane.

Australians love their heritage

There were several epochs in Australia's history during which notable buildings were erected. The convict era, the gold rushes, the good times for wool and wheat, and finally the mineral booms of the twentieth century have all produced important architecture. Australia also has many buildings which celebrate or reflect the times in which they were constructed, from humble city labourers' cottages to magnificent rural station homesteads. Sovereign Hill, at Ballarat, is one of several places which re-create a whole era, in this case the exciting days of the Victorian gold rushes.

Australians have become more aware of their country's history and the worth of historical artefacts, including buildings. More and more architectural treasures are being saved from neglect or destruction and restored to their former grandeur.

Sovereign Hill re-creates the gold rush days in Ballarat, Victoria.

The Princess Theatre in Melbourne has been magnificently restored and refurbished to stage popular hits.

Fremantle in Western Australia is a city which enjoys sharing its nineteenth century heritage with the world.

The hotel at Silverton, a mining ghost town near Broken Hill, New South Wales.

Australians love their outback heritage

The Australian Stockman's Hall of Fame, Longreach, Queensland.

The Matilda Highway meanders north–south through outback Queensland from the Gulf of Carpentaria to the New South Wales border. Roughly in the middle, it runs through the dry, grassy plains of the Longreach-Winton region. The highway is named for possibly Australia's best known song, "Waltzing Matilda", by Banjo Paterson, which had its first public reading in Winton in 1895.

This is ancient country, harbouring evidence of prehistoric animals, and the art and lifestyles of its earliest inhabitants, the Aborigines. The district, sheep country to the north and east and cattle country to the south and west, has a proud history of enterprise and endurance. The first board meeting of Qantas airline was held in Winton in 1921 and its first operational base was in Longreach. The Stockman's Hall of Fame and Outback Heritage Centre in Longreach pays tribute to the pioneers, the stockmen and women, the artists, poets, writers and songwriters who have lived and recorded the history of the outback. Nowadays, mustering is often done from the saddle of a motorbike rather than of a horse, but horses are still part of outback life. One of the most gruelling tests of horse and rider is the annual 250 kilometre Winton to Longreach Hall of Fame endurance ride.

Droving cattle across the plains of outback Australia.

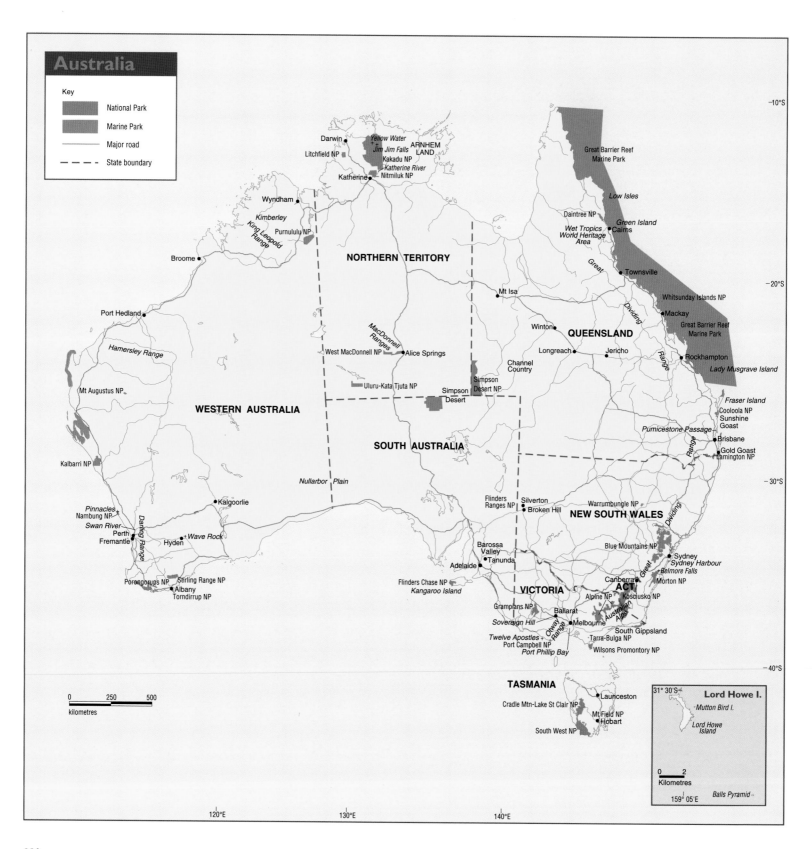

Australia

Key

National Park

Marine Park

Major road

State boundary

Darwin
Yellow Water
Jim Jim Falls
Litchfield NP
Kakadu NP
Katherine River
Katherine
Nitmiluk NP
ARNHEM LAND

Wyndham
Kimberley
King Leopold Range
Purnululu NP

Broome

Port Hedland

Hamersley Range

Mt Augustus NP

WESTERN AUSTRALIA

Kalbarri NP

Kalgoorlie

Nullarbor Plain

Pinnacles
Nambung NP
Swan River
Perth
Fremantle
Hyden
Wave Rock
Darling Range

Porongorups NP
Stirling Range NP
Albany
Torndirrup NP

NORTHERN TERRITORY

Mt Isa

MacDonnell Ranges
West MacDonnell NP
Alice Springs

Uluru-Kata Tjuta NP

Simpson Desert NP
Simpson Desert

SOUTH AUSTRALIA

Channel Country

Winton

Longreach

Jericho

Great Barrier Reef Marine Park

Low Isles

Daintree NP
Green Island
Cairns
Wet Tropics World Heritage Area

Townsville

Whitsunday Islands NP
Mackay
Great Barrier Reef Marine Park

QUEENSLAND

Rockhampton

Lady Musgrave Island

Fraser Island
Cooloola NP
Sunshine Coast
Pumicestone Passage
Brisbane
Gold Coast
Lamington NP

Flinders Ranges NP
Silverton
Broken Hill

Warrumbungle NP

NEW SOUTH WALES

Barossa Valley
Tanunda
Adelaide

Flinders Chase NP
Kangaroo Island

Blue Mountains NP
Sydney
Sydney Harbour
Belmore Falls
Canberra
ACT
Kosciusko NP
Morton NP

Grampians NP
Ballarat
Sovereign Hill
Melbourne
Twelve Apostles
Port Campbell NP
Port Phillip Bay
Otway Range
Alpine NP
Australian Alps
South Gippsland
Tarra-Bulga NP
Wilsons Promontory NP

VICTORIA

Great Dividing Range

TASMANIA

Launceston
Cradle Mtn-Lake St Clair NP
Mt Field NP
Hobart
South West NP

0 250 500
kilometres

−10°S

−20°S

−30°S

−40°S

120°E

130°E

140°E

Lord Howe I.
31° 30'S
Mutton Bird I.
Lord Howe Island

0 2
Kilometres
159° 05'E
Balls Pyramid

112

Exploring Australia

There have never been so many ways to discover Australia's unique landscapes and seascapes, its cities and towns and its fascinating plants and wildlife. All over the continent, there are experts eager to organise horseback rides into the headwaters of the Snowy River, or camel rides across the sand dunes of the Red Centre, or climbing in the Grampians, or scuba diving on the Great Barrier Reef, or whitewater rafting in wild rainforest rivers, or caving beneath the Nullarbor Plain.

Sometimes, however, the simplest way to travel is the most satisfying and many people prefer to organise their own expeditions of discovery. They explore a capital city, escape to the outback, wander through the wild beauties of National Parks, swap stories with the locals, make friends with other travellers and spend extra time where they find something of special interest.

However you choose to explore Australia, safe, happy travelling and may your discoveries enrich your life.

Steve Parish

World-famous photographer Steve Parish began his remarkable career by recording marine life off Australia's coasts. After discovering the fascinations of the rainforest and its wild creatures, he has spent much of his life journeying around Australia photographing the landscapes, plants, animals and the people of the land. Of recent years, he has extended the range of his subjects to include Australia's cities and towns.

The magnificent library of images which has resulted has become the heart of Steve Parish Publishing Pty Ltd. Through the firm's publications, Steve and his wife and partner Jan are realising their dream of sharing Australia with the world.

Celebrating Australia is a collection of titles which present the incomparable beauty of the southern continent in superb photographs and text. As Steve comments: "After a lifetime of travel and asking questions, I have only just begun to discover how much there is to learn about Australia. I hope these books arouse in others a desire like mine to explore and to appreciate this wonderful country."

Index

First published by Steve Parish Publishing Pty Ltd
PO Box 1058, Archerfield BC, Queensland 4108 Australia
© copyright Steve Parish Publishing Pty Ltd
ISBN 1 74021 017 4
Designed and produced by Steve Parish and the Steve Parish Publishing Studio, Brisbane, Australia

Photography: Steve Parish
Text: Pat Slater, Steve Parish Publishing, Australia
Map supplied by MAPgraphics, Brisbane, Australia